AUGUST STRINDBERG

Born in Stockholm in 1849, Strindberg studied medicine at
the University of Uppsala, but soon turned to writing plays. As
assistant librarian at the Royal Library, his personal affairs –
and his creativity as a writer – took on an intensity which
persisted throughout his life. As novels –*The Red Room, Son
of a Servant* – and plays – *Master Olof, The Father, Comrades* –
poured out of him, he fell in love with the first of a succession
of women, many of them actresses. Siri von Essen divorced her
husband to marry Strindberg in 1877 and had three children
by him. As their marriage deteriorated, she probably provided
the inspiration for *Miss Julie*, which premiered in Copenhagen
in 1889, only to be closed down by the Danish censor.

In 1890 *The Father* was staged in Berlin, where Strindberg had
settled after divorcing Siri. There he met Frida Uhl, marrying
her in 1893 but almost immediately falling out with her.
Returning to Sweden, he began work on the autobiographical
Inferno, and in 1898 completed the first part of what was to
become his dramatic trilogy, *To Damascus*. He met his third
wife, the Norwegian actress Harriet Bosse, in 1900: in the
spate of creativity that followed, he wrote *Easter, The Dance of
Death* and *A Dream Play* (written in 1901, published in 1902),
and then divorced her. Many of his plays remained unstaged
until the early 1900s. The first public performance in Sweden
of *Miss Julie* came in 1906. It was directed by August Falck,
with whom Strindberg set up the experimental Intimate
Theatre. He quickly created a repertoire of 'chamber' plays
for the new theatre: *The Storm, After the Fire, The Ghost Sonata*
and *The Pelican*. None met with much success, and when *The
Great Highway* flopped badly, a row with Falck ended with the
closure of the theatre in December 1910.

Strindberg died of stomach cancer in 1912. Earlier that year,
his birthda had been a occasion for popular expression
through St ockholm that earned him
the title of prophet

CARYL CHURCHILL

Caryl Churchill has written for the stage, television and radio. Her stage plays include *Owners* (Royal Court Theatre Upstairs, 1972); *Objections to Sex and Violence* (Royal Court, 1975); *Light Shining in Buckinghamshire* (Joint Stock on tour incl. Theatre Upstairs, 1976); *Vinegar Tom* (Monstrous Regiment on tour, incl. Half Moon and ICA, 1976); *Traps* (Theatre Upstairs, 1977), *Cloud Nine* (Joint Stock on tour incl. Royal Court, London, 1979, then Theatre de Lys, New York, 1981); *Three More Sleepless Nights* (Soho Poly and Theatre Upstairs, 1980); *Top Girls* (Royal Court, London, then Public Theatre, New York, 1982); *Fen* (Joint Stock on tour, incl. Almeida and Royal Court, London, then Public Theatre, New York, 1983); *Softcops* (RSC at the Pit, 1984); *A Mouthful of Birds* with David Lan (Joint Stock on tour, incl. Royal Court, 1986); *Serious Money* (Royal Court and Wyndham's, London, then Public Theatre, New York, 1987); *Icecream* (Royal Court, 1989); *Mad Forest* (Central School of Speech and Drama, then Royal Court, 1990); *Lives of the Great Poisoners* with Orlando Gough and Ian Spink (Second Stride on tour, incl. Riverside Studios, London, 1991); *The Skriker* (Royal National Theatre, 1994); *Thyestes* translated from Seneca (Royal Court Theatre Upstairs, 1994); *Hotel* with Orlando Gough and Ian Spink (Second Stride on tour, incl. The Place, London, 1997); *This is a Chair* (London International Festival of Theatre at the Royal Court, 1997); *Blue Heart* (Joint Stock on tour, incl. Royal Court Theatre, 1997); *Far Away* (Royal Court Theatre Upstairs, 2000, and Albery, London, 2001, then New York Theatre Workshop, 2002); *A Number* (Royal Court Theatre Downstairs, 2002, then New York Theatre Workshop, 2004).

AUGUST STRINDBERG

A DREAM PLAY

in a new version by

CARYL CHURCHILL

from a literal translation by Charlotte Barslund
with an Introduction by Caryl Churchill

NICK HERN BOOKS
London

www.nickhernbooks.co.uk

A Nick Hern Book

A Dream Play first published in 2005 as a paperback original
by Nick Hern Books, 14 Larden Road, London W3 7ST

This version of *A Dream Play* copyright 2005 © Caryl Churchill Ltd
Introduction copyright 2005 © Caryl Churchill Ltd

Translation of Strindberg's Author's Note copyright 2005
© Charlotte Barslund

This version is from a literal translation by Charlotte Barslund

Caryl Churchill has asserted her right to be identified as
the translator of this work

Cover design: '*On Being an Angel*, Providence, Rhode Island,
1975-1978' by Francesca Woodman. Courtesy Betty and
George Woodman

Typeset by Country Setting, Kingsdown, Kent, CT14 8ES
Printed and bound in Great Britain by Bookmarque, Croydon,
Surrey

A CIP catalogue record for this book is available from
the British Library

ISBN 1 85459 851 1

Introduction

Is it a larder? Is it a fridge? Is it more fun, more vivid, or
even more true to what Strindberg meant, to update the
larder door which is just like the ones the Officer saw when
he was a child? A larder's where the food is, so does a fridge
give us more directly, without archaism, the promise of
satisfaction of appetite? And make it easier to see why the
characters hope that if they finally get the door open they'll
find the meaning of life inside? Or is it a silly idea and a
modernism too far?

You don't of course consciously think all that, you think
'fridge' and smile. I did this version for Katie Mitchell, who
was already planning to direct it at the National Theatre,
and she had said she welcomed anachronisms. So when the
happy couple decide to kill themselves because bliss doesn't
last ('Life is wretched. I pity mankind.'), I could write,
'People are so fucked up.'

There's a strand of the play that is about academia, and
that's where I've done the most updating. The university and
its bossy deans of theology, philosophy, medicine and law
don't have the power over us that they seemed to have over
Strindberg. Here a bishop, psychoanalyst, scientist and
barrister are on the committee of the inquiry looking into
the opening of the door, and the solicitor is refused not a
doctorate but a knighthood. Not a big change, and on the
whole this version stays close to the original.

What I've mostly done is tighten the dialogue and cut out a
few chunks. Strindberg lived in a far more Christian society
than ours, and his swipes at it look a bit unnecessary now, so
I've taken some of them out. Though, with a Christian
prime minister and an American president voted in by right-
wing Christians both calling us to fight evil, perhaps we
should feel as dominated by religion as Strindberg did. Still,
we don't, so I'm not restoring those cuts. I've cut references

to the Flying Dutchman and the Caliph Haroun; I've cut things that seemed repetitive; sometimes I've cut bits that just seemed to me or Katie not to work very well. And I've cut the meaning of life.

When it turns out there's nothing behind the fridge door, the daughter of the gods promises the writer she'll tell him the secret when they're alone. What she says may have seemed more original or daring when Strindberg wrote it, but seems a bit of an anticlimax to us. So in this version she whispers it to the writer and we never know what it is. But was telling us the meaning of life one of the main points of the play for Strindberg? I hope not. I do feel abashed at cutting another writer's work; directors have fewer qualms.

I said the version was close to the original but of course I've no idea what the original is as I don't know any Swedish. The very few translations I've done before have been from French or Latin, where I knew enough to see what the text was literally saying. I'd never wanted to work from a literal translation of a language I didn't know. To my surprise, the one I was given wasn't literally literal, the kind of thing I'd done for myself at first when translating Latin, with odd word order and odd words, but a translation, by Charlotte Barslund, which seemed to me as performable as the existing translations I'd looked at. So that for me is the original I've kept close to.

People who are looking at this text after seeing Katie Mitchell's production may or may not find considerable differences. Working as she has before, she and the actors may add other material or change the order of scenes, or they may end up very close to this text. I've put in Strindberg's stage directions, which are what Katie and designer Vicki Mortimer are starting from, rather than describing their solutions, since other productions may want to use this text and come up with their own versions of stage doors, caves and quarantine stations. When Strindberg was writing the play a castle was being built in Stockholm and grew over the trees, and the town was full of soldiers. The equivalent fast-growing buildings for us are office towers; a soldier means our current wars to us, not the romantic officer of the play; our city towers are full of businessmen. So we've gone for a tower, which works well both ways – prisoners are kept in towers – and for a while we went with a Banker instead of an Officer. Katie's staying with the Banker but I've gone back to the Officer for this text, feeling as with the stage directions that I shouldn't put too much of the production into it. I've kept the fridge though – if you're not happy with anachronism feel free to go back to the larder.

I'd read the play several times over the years, admired the way it moved, but never, I realise, taken in the detail. I was surprised by its tenderness. Since starting this version I've learned more about Strindberg than I knew before. I suppose I'd thought of him as misogynistic and depressive and mostly concerned with miserable relationships and disastrous families. All of which of course you can find in *A Dream Play*. I hadn't realised how political he was, that he was a hero to trade unionists, who made a detour in a parade to pass his window. When asked what mattered to him most he said, 'Disarmament.' He added the coal-miner scene (building workers here) after the play was finished, because there was a miners' strike in Stockholm.

I'm not sure how I'd feel if someone treated one of my plays the way I've treated Strindberg's, even though I hope I've made it clearer and not spoilt it. I wouldn't like it now, but perhaps when a play is over a hundred years old you should just be glad it's still being done. And it survives unharmed in Swedish. I'd like to think he'd be glad about this version. I'd like to make him smile. But maybe he'd say, 'Oh woe. Life is wretched.'

Caryl Churchill

Caryl Churchill's version of *A Dream Play*, with additional material by Katie Mitchell and the Company, was first performed in the Cottosloe auditorium of the National Theatre, London, on 15 February 2005 (previews from 4 February). The cast was as follows:

Mark Arends
Anastasia Hille
Kristin Hutchinson
Sean Jackson
Charlotte Roach
Dominic Rowan
Justin Salinger
Susie Trayling
Lucy Whybrow
Angus Wright

Director   Katie Mitchell
Designer   Vicki Mortimer
Lighting Designer   Chris Davey
Choreographer   Kate Flatt
Music Director and Arranger   Simon Allen
Sound Designer   Christopher Shutt

A DREAM PLAY

Author's Note

As with his earlier dream play, *To Damascus*, the author has in this dream play sought to imitate the disjointed yet seemingly logical shape of a dream. Everything can happen, everything is possible and probable. Time and place do not exist; the imagination spins, weaving new patterns on a flimsy basis of reality: a mixture of memories, experiences, free associations, absurdities and improvisations.

The characters split, double, multiply, evaporate, condense, dissolve and merge. But one consciousness rules them all: the dreamer's; for him there are no secrets, no inconsistencies, no scruples and no laws. He does not judge or acquit, he merely relates; and, because a dream is usually painful rather than pleasant, a tone of melancholy and compassion for all living creatures permeates the rambling narrative. Sleep, the liberator, often feels like torture, but when the torment is at its worst, the moment of awakening comes and reconciles the sufferer with reality, which, regardless of how painful it might be, is at this very moment a joy compared to the agonies of dreaming.

August Strindberg

4

Characters

AGNES, DAUGHTER OF THE GODS
GLAZIER

OFFICER
OFFICER'S FATHER AND MOTHER
LINA, THEIR MAID

STAGE DOOR KEEPER
BILLSTICKER
VICTORIA
SINGER
DANCER
PROMPTER
THEATRE PEOPLE
POLICEMEN

SOLICITOR
KRISTIN

RICH FAT SICK
QUARANTINE MASTER
WRITER
HE
SHE

MAIDS
EDITH
HER MOTHER
LIEUTENANT
ALICE
TEACHER
BOYS
NEWLYWEDS
BLIND MAN
TWO BUILDING WORKERS
LADY AND GENTLEMAN
CREW

CHAIR OF INQUIRY
BISHOP
PSYCHOANALYST
SCIENTIST
BARRISTER

1. Outside the Tower

Huge hollyhocks.

A tower with a flower bud on top.

AGNES *and* GLAZIER.

AGNES	Look how the tower's grown.
GLAZIER	What tower?
AGNES	It's twice the size it was last year.
GLAZIER	Yes of course, it must be the fertiliser.
AGNES	But shouldn't it be flowering by now?
GLAZIER	Can't you see the flower?
AGNES	Yes, yes, I see it. Do you know who lives in the tower?
GLAZIER	I do but I can't remember.
AGNES	I think it's a prisoner. And I think he's waiting for me to set him free. Let's go in.

2. Room inside the Tower

AGNES, GLAZIER, OFFICER.

OFFICER *is rocking his chair and hitting the table with his sword.*

AGNES	(*Takes the sword.*) Don't. Don't.
OFFICER	Please, Agnes, let me keep my sword.
AGNES	You're hacking the table. (*To* GLAZIER.)

Go down to the tackroom and mend the window and I'll see you later.

GLAZIER *goes*.

You're a prisoner and I've come to set you free.

OFFICER   It's what I've been waiting for. But I wasn't sure you wanted to.

AGNES   Do you want to?

OFFICER   I don't know. I'll be miserable either way. It's terrible sitting here but it's going to be so painful being free. Agnes, I'd rather stay here if I can go on seeing you.

AGNES   What do you see?

OFFICER   I look at you and it's something to do with the stars and the smallest particles, you're somehow connected.

AGNES   But so are you.

OFFICER   Then why do I have to muck out the horses?

AGNES   To make you long to get away.

OFFICER   I do but it's such an effort.

AGNES   It's your duty to seek freedom in the light.

OFFICER   To be free is a duty?

AGNES   Your duty to life.

OFFICER   Life doesn't do its duty to me so why should I?

AGNES, OFFICER, FATHER, MOTHER.

MOTHER *is working on shirts at a table*.

FATHER gives MOTHER a silk dress.

FATHER   You don't want it?

MOTHER   What's the point when I'm dying?

FATHER   You believe the doctor?

MOTHER   I believe how I feel.

FATHER   Then it is serious? And all you think about is how it affects the children.

MOTHER   They're all that matters.

FATHER   Kristina, forgive me. For everything.

MOTHER   Oh yes? All right, forgive me too. We've both hurt each other. We don't know why. We couldn't help it. Look, here are the boys' new shirts. They have clean ones on Wednesdays and Sundays. And make sure Lina washes them all over. Are you going out?

FATHER   I have to be at college. It's nearly eleven.

MOTHER   Get Alfred for me first.

FATHER   But he's here already.

MOTHER   My eyes must be going. Or it's getting dark.

She turns on the light.

Alfred.

FATHER *goes.*

Who's that girl?

OFFICER   Agnes.

MOTHER   Oh is that Agnes? You know what they're saying? She's the daughter of the gods and she's come down to earth to find out what it's like to be a human being. But don't say anything.

Alfred, before I die. Always remember this.

OFFICER   Yes.

MOTHER   Don't go on feeling life's been unfair to you.

OFFICER   But it has.

MOTHER   You were punished for stealing a coin that had just slipped down the back of the sofa.

OFFICER   Yes and it ruined my life.

MOTHER   Now go to the cupboard.

OFFICER   You know about that?

MOTHER   Treasure Island.

OFFICER   Don't.

MOTHER   Which your brother was punished for when it was you who tore it to pieces and hid it in the cupboard.

OFFICER   How can that cupboard be there after twenty years? We've moved house. And you died ten years ago.

MOTHER   So? You're always asking questions and ruining everything. Look, here's Lina.

LINA *enters.*

LINA   Thank you for giving me time off, ma'am, but I can't go anyway because I've nothing to wear.

MOTHER   Here, borrow this.

LINA   Oh ma'am, I couldn't.

MOTHER   Don't be silly. I won't be going out any more.

OFFICER   What will dad say? It was a present.

MOTHER   Alfred, that's so petty.

FATHER pops his head round.

FATHER   Are you lending my present to the maid?

MOTHER   Don't say maid like that, I was a maid once or have you forgotten? Why do you have to be so horrible to the poor girl?

FATHER   Why do you have to be so horrible to your husband?

MOTHER   Whenever you try to help someone you hurt someone else. I'm sick of life.

MOTHER turns off the light.

AGNES, OFFICER.

AGNES   I'm sorry for them.

OFFICER   Really?

AGNES   Yes, people find things so difficult. But there's always love. Look.

3. Outside the Stage Door

Enormous foxglove.

Green tree.

Fridge door.

Billboard.

AGNES, OFFICER, STAGE DOOR KEEPER, BILLSTICKER.

STAGE DOOR KEEPER *is sewing.*

AGNES   Is that the same star blanket you're still making?

SD KEEPER   Twenty-six years isn't long.

AGNES   And he never came back?

SD KEEPER   It wasn't his fault.

AGNES   (*To* BILLSTICKER.) Didn't she used to be a ballet dancer?

BILLSTICK   Yes, she was a prima ballerina. But when he left, her dancing went with him and she stopped getting the parts.

AGNES   Everyone's complaining. If it's not what they say, it's how they look.

BILLSTICK   I don't, not now I've got my fishing net and my bucket. That's what I wanted when I was four and now I'm fifty-four and I've got them.

AGNES   Fifty years for that.

BILLSTICK   It's a green bucket.

AGNES   (*To* SD KEEPER.) Lend me your coat and I'll sit here and watch.

             She puts on the coat and sits down.

SD KEEPER   It's nearly the end of the season and today they hear if they're going to be kept on.

AGNES   And what if they're not?

SD KEEPER   I hide my face.

             SINGER *crosses in tears.*

             Look, she's been dropped.

AGNES   Poor things.

BILLSTICK   No, this one's happy. He's going to marry
                 Victoria.

                 OFFICER *enters with bunch of roses.*

OFFICER   Victoria!

BILLSTICK   She'll be right down.

OFFICER   The taxi's here, I've booked a table, the
                 champagne's on ice. I have to give you a
                 hug.

                 He hugs STAGE DOOR KEEPER *and*
                 AGNES.

                 Victoria!

VICTORIA   (*Off.*) Coming!

AGNES   Don't you know me?

OFFICER   Sorry, I only know Victoria. I've been
                 walking up and down for seven years. You
                 can see how my feet have worn a path. Ah
                 she's mine. Victoria! (*He waits.*) She's getting
                 dressed. I see you've got a fishing net.
                 Everyone at the opera loves fish even
                 though they can't sing. How much does a
                 thing like that cost?

BILLSTICK   You have to save up.

OFFICER   Victoria! (*Of tree.*) Look, it's turning green
                 again. Eighth time.

                 Victoria! She's combing her fringe. Excuse
                 me, I have to go up and fetch my bride.

SD KEEPER   No one's allowed in the dressing rooms.

OFFICER   Seven times three hundred and sixty-five
                 is . . . two thousand five hundred and fifty-

five days. And I've looked at this door two thousand five hundred and fifty-five times without knowing where it goes. What is it? Does anyone live there?

SD KEEPER   I don't know. I've never seen it opened.

OFFICER   It looks like a fridge door I saw when I was four and the maid took me out one Sunday afternoon. Different families, different maids, but I never got further than the kitchen and I liked sitting under the table. I've seen so many kitchens and the fridge doors were always the same. But the opera can't have a fridge because it hasn't got a kitchen. Victoria! Listen, I don't suppose she could come out a different way?

SD KEEPER   No, this is the only way out.

OFFICER   Good, then I can't miss her.

THEATRE PEOPLE *come out.*

She'll be here soon. I saw that identical foxglove when I was seven in a vicarage garden. There were two blue pigeons. Then a bee flew into one of the bells and I thought 'got you' and grabbed the flower and the bee stung me right through it and I cried. But then the vicar's wife put wet earth on it and we had wild strawberries and milk for supper. It seems to be getting dark. (*To* BILLSTICKER.) Where are you going?

BILLSTICK   Home to supper.

OFFICER   Evening? Now? Listen, can I use the phone? I have to phone the tower.

AGNES   What for?

OFFICER   I want to tell the glazier to put in double-glazing. It's nearly winter and I feel the cold.

OFFICER goes.

AGNES   Who is Victoria?

BILLSTICK   The one he loves.

AGNES   Yes, that's all he knows about her. He doesn't care about what she means to other people. Just what she is to him, that's all she is.

BILLSTICKER goes.

Suddenly it's dark.

SD KEEPER   Getting dark quickly today.

AGNES   A year can feel like a minute.

SD KEEPER   No, a minute can feel like a year.

OFFICER comes back, dusty, roses withered.

OFFICER   She hasn't come down yet.

SD KEEPER   No.

OFFICER   She will come. She will come. But maybe I'll cancel lunch. Yes, that's what I'll do.

He goes.

SD KEEPER   Can I have my coat now?

AGNES   No, you have a break and I'll stay here. I want to find out more about life.

SD KEEPER   You don't get any sleep in this job.

AGNES   Not at night?

SD KEEPER   You can have a doze if you don't mind being woken up, because the security guards change every three hours.

AGNES	What a horrible job.
SD KEEPER	Plenty of people want it.
AGNES	Want to be woken up?
SD KEEPER	That's not the worse thing, or the cold and the damp. It's hearing all their troubles. There's thirty years of trouble in that coat.
AGNES	It's heavy and scratchy.
SD KEEPER	Call me when it gets too much.
AGNES	Goodbye. If you can bear it, I can.
SD KEEPER	Be kind to them.

STAGE DOOR KEEPER *goes.*

The leaves have fallen from the tree, the foxglove has wilted. OFFICER *enters, his hair and beard are grey, his clothes worn and dirty. The roses are just stems.*

OFFICER   It seems to be autumn. I can tell by the tree. But autumn's spring for me because that's when the theatre opens for the new season. And then she'll come. Do you mind if I sit down for a moment?

AGNES   Please do. I can stand.

OFFICER   If only I could get some sleep it wouldn't be so bad.

I can't stop wondering about this door. What's behind it?

Faint music.

They've started rehearsals.

Alternate light and dark.

What's going on? Light dark, light dark.

AGNES	Day night, day night. So you don't have to wait so long.

BILLSTICKER returns.

OFFICER	Catch anything?
BILLSTICK	Yes, plenty. But the summer was a bit hot and rather long. It's a very good net but not quite what I imagined.
OFFICER	No, this isn't quite what I imagined.
BILLSTICK	She hasn't come?
OFFICER	Not yet, she'll be down in a minute. You don't happen to know what's behind this door?
BILLSTICK	No, I've never seen it open.
OFFICER	I'm going to phone a locksmith.

OFFICER goes.

AGNES	What was wrong with the net?
BILLSTICK	No, it's fine. But it wasn't quite what I imagined. I did enjoy it but . . .
AGNES	How did you imagine it?
BILLSTICK	It's hard to say.
AGNES	Maybe green but not exactly that green?
BILLSTICK	That's why everyone likes talking to you. Could you spare a few minutes?
AGNES	Come in here and tell me.

Tree green again and foxglove in bloom.

OFFICER enters, old with white hair, worn shoes, carrying stems.

BALLET DANCER *enters.*

OFFICER	Has Victoria left?
DANCER	No, not yet.
OFFICER	Then I'll wait. I expect she'll be down soon.
DANCER	I expect so.
OFFICER	Don't go, I've sent for the locksmith, you'll see what's behind this door.
DANCER	That's interesting. That and the tower that keeps growing. Do you know the tower?
OFFICER	I was a prisoner there.
DANCER	Really? were you?

SINGER *enters.*

OFFICER	Has Victoria left?
SINGER	No, she never leaves.
OFFICER	That's because she loves me. Please don't go. There's a locksmith coming to open the door.
SINGER	Opening the door? what fun. There's just something I want to ask the stage-door keeper.

PROMPTER *enters.*

OFFICER	Has Victoria left?
PROMPTER	Not as far as I know.
OFFICER	There, didn't I tell you she was waiting for me? Don't go, we're about to open the door.
PROMPTER	Which door?

OFFICER   Is there more than one door?

PROMPTER   Oh this one. Yes, I'll stay to see that. Just
               need to have a word with the stage-door
               keeper.

               GLAZIER *enters.*

OFFICER   Is that the locksmith?

GLAZIER   No, he had friends round, but a glazier's
               just as good.

OFFICER   Yes, of course. Did you bring your
               diamond? Let's do it.

               More SINGERS *and* DANCERS *enter in
               opera costumes.*

               Thank you all for coming. This is a once in
               a lifetime moment, so I ask you to –

               Armed POLICEMEN *enter, shouting.*

POLICE   Keep away from the door.

OFFICER   Oh god, whenever you try to do something
               new. But we'll see them in court. A
               solicitor!

4. Room (Solicitor's Office)

AGNES, OFFICER, SOLICITOR.

SOLICITOR   Let me take your coat. I'll put it in the bin.

AGNES   Not yet. I know it's disgusting because it's
               full of people's problems but I want to get
               even more. I'd like to soak up all the
               crimes you know about and the false
               imprisonments and abuse.

SOLICITOR   Your coat's not big enough. The pain's
              spattered all over the room, it's stained the
              wallpaper. It's all over me, my hands are
              black, look they're cracked and bleeding.
              I can only wear my clothes a couple of
              days and then they stink. I use air freshener
              but it's no good. I sleep here as well and all
              my dreams are violent. I'm in the middle of
              a murder trial now, but that's all right. Do
              you know what's worse? Divorce. When
              you think how they started out full of
              wonder and love, and they go on for pages
              and pages accusing each other and making
              themselves out to be right. And if someone
              just kindly and simply asked them what it's
              really all about they wouldn't know. They
              quarrelled about a green salad. They
              quarrelled about a word. They quarrelled
              about nothing. But the pain. Look at me.
              No woman's going to want me after all this.
              No one even wants to be friends with me.

AGNES   I'm so sorry.

SOLICITOR   You should be. And what do people live
              on? They don't earn enough to get married
              so they're always in debt. (*To* OFFICER.)
              What do you want?

OFFICER   I just wanted to ask if Victoria's left.

SOLICITOR   No, she definitely hasn't. Why are you
              pointing at my cupboard?

OFFICER   I thought the door looked like . . .

SOLICITOR   Oh no no no.

              Bells.

OFFICER   Is it a funeral?

SOLICITOR   No, it's an honours ceremony. And I'm
              going to be given an honour. Would you
              like to be knighted for something or other?

OFFICER   Yes, why not. It's something to do.

Ceremony.

SOLICITOR *goes forward but is refused.*

AGNES *enters. The coat is clean.*

AGNES   Look how clean it is. But what's the matter? Didn't you get it?

SOLICITOR   I'm not good enough.

AGNES   Why? because you do legal aid? because you get people off? and if they're found guilty you get them shorter sentences. Some criminals do do terrible things of course but I'm still sorry for them.

SOLICITOR   Don't say anything against them. I'll always defend them.

AGNES   But why do they hurt each other?

SOLICITOR   They can't help it.

AGNES   Maybe we could make them better. Together.

SOLICITOR   No one's going to listen to us. If only the gods knew what it's like.

AGNES   They will, I promise. Do you know what I can see in this mirror? The world the right way round. Because usually it's the wrong way round.

SOLICITOR   How did it get the wrong way round?

AGNES   When it was copied.

SOLICITOR   Yes, I always thought there was something wrong with the copy. I sometimes think there's an original which was much better and then I feel really depressed. Everyone does. Like a glass splinter in your eye.

AGNES   Let me play for you.

                   She plays organ but we hear voices.

VOICES   Whoever's up there
                   have mercy on us
                   save us and spare us
                   please don't be angry.

5. Cave

SOLICITOR, AGNES.

SOLICITOR   Where are we?

AGNES   What can you hear?

SOLICITOR   Drips. Drops.

AGNES   Tears. What else?

SOLICITOR   Sighs. Wailing.

AGNES   So why all this complaining? What's it
                   about? Don't people enjoy anything?

SOLICITOR   Love. They do like love. A partner and a
                   home.

AGNES   Can I try it?

SOLICITOR   With me?

AGNES   With you. You know all the mistakes we
                   mustn't make.

SOLICITOR   I'm poor.

AGNES   That doesn't matter so long as we love
                   each other. And beauty doesn't cost
                   anything.

SOLICITOR   There are things I hate, and you might turn out to like them.

AGNES   Then we'll both have to change a bit.

SOLICITOR   And what if we get tired of each other?

AGNES   We'll have a baby.

SOLICITOR   Would you really have me? poor, ugly? a failure?

AGNES   Yes, let's share our lives.

SOLICITOR   Let's do that.

6. Room (One-Room Flat at Solicitor's)

AGNES, KRISTIN.

KRISTIN *is pasting the windows shut to keep out draughts.*

KRISTIN   Pasting, pasting.

AGNES   You're shutting out the air. I'm suffocating.

KRISTIN   There's just one little crack left.

AGNES   I can't breathe.

KRISTIN   Pasting, pasting.

SOLICITOR *enters.*

SOLICITOR   That's good, Kristin. It saves money on heating.

AGNES   It's as if you're sticking my mouth together.

SOLICITOR   Is she asleep?

AGNES   At last.

SOLICITOR	All that screaming drives away the clients.
AGNES	What can we do?
SOLICITOR	Nothing.
AGNES	We need a bigger place.
SOLICITOR	We can't afford it.
AGNES	Do you mind if I open the window? I can't breathe.
SOLICITOR	You'll let the heat out, it's too cold.
AGNES	I know, let's scrub the office so it looks better.
SOLICITOR	You haven't got the strength and nor have I, and Kristin has to keep pasting, she's got to paste the whole building tight, every crack in the ceiling, the floor, the walls.
AGNES	I don't mind being poor. I just don't like dirt.
SOLICITOR	Being poor can lead to dirt.
AGNES	It's worse than the worst I imagined.
SOLICITOR	Things aren't too bad. We've plenty to eat.
AGNES	Lentils?
SOLICITOR	Lentils are good for you.
AGNES	I hate lentils.
SOLICITOR	Why didn't you say so?
AGNES	I was trying to put up with it because I love you.
SOLICITOR	Then I must give up lentils. We both have to change.

AGNES	What can we eat? Fish? You hate fish.
SOLICITOR	Fish is expensive.
AGNES	This is harder than I expected.
SOLICITOR	You see? And the baby, who should make us closer, just makes things worse.
AGNES	Beloved, I'm going to die in this air, in this room, looking down on the backyard, the baby screaming all night, no sleep, the neighbours shouting. I'm going to die.
SOLICITOR	Poor little flower. No light, no air.
AGNES	And you say there are people who are worse off.
SOLICITOR	I'm one of the lucky ones.
AGNES	I think I'd be all right if I had something beautiful.
SOLICITOR	I know you want flowers, you want that azalea you saw in the shop, but it costs as much as forty pounds of potatoes.
AGNES	I'd go without food if I could have a flower.
SOLICITOR	There is a kind of beauty you can have for nothing. And not having it really hurts if you're a man who loves beauty.
AGNES	What is it?
SOLICITOR	You'll be angry.
AGNES	We've agreed we'll never get angry.
SOLICITOR	Yes, we've agreed we can say anything to each other but not in that angry voice. Do you know what I mean? You've never heard it, have you?

AGNES   You'll never hear it from me.

SOLICITOR   And never from me.

AGNES   So say it.

SOLICITOR   Well, when I go into someone's house, the
               first thing I notice is how the curtains hang.
               If any of the hooks are missing, I walk out.
               Then I look at the chairs. If they're
               straight, I'll stay. Then I look at the lamps.
               If the shades are askew, the whole house is
               off-balance. And this is the beauty you can
               have for nothing.

AGNES   Not in that tone of voice.

SOLICITOR   It wasn't.

AGNES   Yes it was.

SOLICITOR   For god's sake.

AGNES   What did you say?

SOLICITOR   I'm sorry, Agnes. But I mind your
               untidiness just as much as you mind the
               dirt. And I didn't like to do any tidying up
               in case you thought I was criticising. Ugh.
               Shall we stop this?

AGNES   Marriage is really difficult, isn't it? You
               have to be an angel.

SOLICITOR   Yes, ideally.

AGNES   I might start hating you after this.

SOLICITOR   That would be horrible. But let's see it
               coming and not let it happen. I'll never say
               anything about untidiness again. Though I
               do hate it.

AGNES   And I'll eat lentil soup though I hate that.

SOLICITOR So a life of what we hate. That's going to be fun.

AGNES I'm really sorry for people.

SOLICITOR You see?

AGNES Yes but let's try to find a way through. We can see what the problems are.

SOLICITOR Yes, we're intelligent enough to understand each other.

AGNES If little things go wrong we can have a laugh.

SOLICITOR Of course we can. I saw something this morning in the paper – where is the paper?

AGNES What paper?

SOLICITOR Do we get more than one paper?

AGNES Laugh about it. And not that tone of voice. I used it to wrap up the potato peelings when I threw them away.

SOLICITOR Oh for god's sake.

AGNES Please smile. There was an article which made me really upset.

SOLICITOR And which I agreed with. Well. I'll smile, I'll smile till you see my back teeth. I'll be nice and not say what I think and agree to everything and pretend. So you threw away my paper. I see. Look, I'm tidying up again which makes you angry. Agnes, this is impossible.

AGNES Yes, it is.

SOLICITOR But we've got to stay together because of the baby.

AGNES	You're right. For the baby. Oh. Oh. We've got to stay together.
SOLICITOR	And now it's time to go and see some clients, who are all desperate for me to keep them out of prison and make someone else go instead. They're beside themselves.
AGNES	Poor poor people. And the pasting.
KRISTIN	Pasting. Pasting.

SOLICITOR *is fiddling with the door.*

AGNES	Don't make the bolt squeak. It's as if you're squeezing my heart.
SOLICITOR	Squeezing. Squeezing.
AGNES	Don't do it.
SOLICITOR	Squeezing.
AGNES	No.
SOLICITOR	Squeez –

OFFICER *enters and adjusts the bolt.*

OFFICER	Allow me.
SOLICITOR	Please. Since you've got a knighthood.
OFFICER	Yes, life's all before me. Fame and glory.
SOLICITOR	What will you live on?
OFFICER	Live on?
SOLICITOR	Don't you need a home? clothes? food?
OFFICER	That all sorts itself out so long as someone loves you.
SOLICITOR	I suppose so. I suppose so. Paste, Kristin. Paste till they can't breathe.

SOLICITOR *goes out.*

KRISTIN   Pasting. Pasting till they can't breathe.

OFFICER   Will you come away with me?

AGNES   Yes but where to?

OFFICER   The seaside. It's summer there. Sunshine, flowers, children –

AGNES   I want to go.

OFFICER   Come on.

SOLICITOR *comes back.*

SOLICITOR   Look, hairpins all over the floor again.

OFFICER   He's noticed the hairpins too.

SOLICITOR   As well as what? Look, two sides, one pin. Two and one. If I straighten it out, it's one. If I bend it it's two but it's still one. It means 'these two are one.' But if I snap it – then they're two, two.

OFFICER   To break it the prongs have to go apart. If they get closer, it holds.

SOLICITOR   And if they're parallel they never meet.

OFFICER   It's perfect and impossible. A straight line which is two parallels.

SOLICITOR   A bolt which locks when it's open. And when I close the door, I open a way out for you, Agnes.

SOLICITOR *goes.*

AGNES   So?

7. Quarantine Station by the Sea

Scorched earth.

Pigsties.

In the distance, on the other side of the bay, a beautiful seashore, villas, boats.

RICH FAT SICK *exercising on machines like instruments of torture.*

AGNES, OFFICER, QUARANTINE MASTER.

QUARANTINE MASTER *is wearing a monster mask.*

OFFICER	We're in the wrong place.
Q MASTER	Aren't you the one who's waiting outside the theatre?
OFFICER	Yes, I am.
Q MASTER	Have you got the door open yet?
OFFICER	No, we're still in the middle of the appeal. The billsticker's gone off with his net so it's taking a while to get all the evidence. But the glazier's put new windows in the tower and it's grown another ten floors. It's been a good year for growing, hot and wet.
Q MASTER	Not as hot as here.
OFFICER	How hot do you keep your furnaces then?
Q MASTER	Sixty centigrade to disinfect for cholera.
OFFICER	Cholera? is there cholera?
Q MASTER	Didn't you know?
OFFICER	Yes, I do know of course, but I forget about it.

Q MASTER   I wish I could forget. What I'd really like is to forget myself. That's why I go to parties.

OFFICER   Why, what's happened to you?

Q MASTER   If I talk about it they say I'm boasting and if I don't they say I'm a hypocrite.

OFFICER   Is that why you dress up as a monster?

Q MASTER   Yes, just a little more monstrous than I am.

OFFICER   Who's this?

Q MASTER   A writer with an appointment for a mud bath. It gives him a thick skin.

Enter WRITER.

WRITER   Lina.

LINA *enters.*

Lina, let Miss Agnes have a look at you. She knew you ten years ago when you were young, happy and even pretty. Look at her now. Five children, hunger, beatings. All that beauty destroyed by duty, which we're told produces inner tranquillity reflected in the −

Q MASTER   Shut up, shut up.

AGNES   Tell me what's wrong.

LINA   I'll get into trouble.

AGNES   Who's cruel to you?

LINA   I'll get a beating.

WRITER   That's what it's like, Agnes.

OFFICER   Visitors.

HE *and* SHE *are passing in a boat.*

Look, perfect happiness. Young love.

HE *sings.*

HE   When I was a child
            I was lonely here.
            Same sea, same woods, same
            sky, same sun, but all
            new now with my love.

OFFICER   It's Victoria.

Q MASTER   What?

OFFICER   It's his Victoria. I still have my own.
            Raise the quarantine flag. I'll pull them in.

            QUARANTINE MASTER *waves a yellow
            flag.*

            OFFICER *tugs a rope, pulling the boat in.*

            Hold it.

            HE *and* SHE *react to quarantine station with
            disgust.*

Q MASTER   Yes yes, of course you don't like it. But all
            passengers arriving from infected areas have
            to land here.

WRITER   How can you do this to people in love?
            Don't touch them.

HE   What have we done wrong?

Q MASTER   Nothing. You can still have a bad time.

SHE   We'd only just started to be happy.

HE   How long do we have to wait?

Q MASTER   Six weeks.

SHE   Then we'd rather go home.

HE   We can't stay here. Scorched earth.

WRITER   Don't worry, you're in love. And that's even stronger than sulphur.

Q MASTER   I'm lighting the sulphur now. This way please.

SHE   My dress isn't colourfast.

Q MASTER   No, it's going to turn white. And so will the roses.

HE   So will your face. In six weeks.

SHE   (*To* OFFICER.) I suppose you're happy now.

OFFICER   No. Not really. Seeing you happy did make me feel a bit low but I've got a knighthood now so I've got that status, ha ha, oh yes. And this autumn I'll start teaching. Teaching boys what I learned all through my childhood. And now I'll teach it all my adult life and all my old age, the same stuff. What's twice two? How many times does two go into four? Till I get my pension and wander round with nothing to do, waiting for meals and newspapers till I'm taken off to the crematorium to be burnt. And Victoria, whom I loved and wanted to be happy, she is happy and that makes me miserable.

SHE   So how can I be happy? Perhaps you'll feel better while I'm a prisoner here. Does that help?

OFFICER   I can't be happy if you're miserable. Oh.

HE   And how can I be happy now I realise what I've done to you?

OFFICER   I'm sorry for all of us. Oh.

ALL THREE   Oh.

AGNES   Life's really difficult. I'm sorry for all of
               them.

ALL THREE   Oh.

8. Outside a Ballroom by the Sea

The quarantine station is in the distance on the other side of the bay.

MAIDS *are outside watching the dancing through a window.*

Ugly EDITH *is sitting outside.*

A piano.
A yellow house.
Children in summer clothes playing.
A jetty with boats and flags.
In the bay, a warship.
Bare trees and snow.

AGNES *and* OFFICER *enter.*

AGNES   This is the place we meant to come to.
               Every day's a holiday and parties start in
               the morning. (*To* MAIDS.) Why don't you
               go inside and dance?

MAIDS   Us?

OFFICER   They're the help.

AGNES   Oops. But why isn't Edith dancing?

               EDITH *hides face in hands.*

OFFICER   Don't ask. She's been sitting in there for
               three hours and nobody's asked her to
               dance.

               OFFICER *goes into the yellow house.*

AGNES   Parties are a cruel kind of fun.

MOTHER *in party dress comes out of the ballroom.*

MOTHER   Why don't you come inside? I keep telling you.

EDITH   I know I'm ugly and no one wants to dance with me but I don't have to sit in there offering myself.

EDITH *plays the piano – Bach Toccata con Fuga 10. Music from ballroom rises to compete, then is drowned out by it.* GUESTS *come out of the ballroom and everyone listens to her playing.*

Naval LIEUTENANT *seizes* ALICE, *one of the guests, and takes her off to the jetty.*

LIEUTENANT Come on, quick.

EDITH *stops playing.*

In the yellow house.

SCHOOLBOYS, OFFICER *sitting among them,* TEACHER.

TEACHER   Twice two.

OFFICER *can't remember.*

Stand up when I ask you a question.

OFFICER   Twice two. I think . . . It's two two.

TEACHER   So you didn't do your homework?

OFFICER   Yes I did. I do know it. I can't say it.

TEACHER   You know it but can't say it? Maybe I can help you. (*Pulls his hair.*)

OFFICER   This is terrible.

TEACHER   It's terrible that a big boy like you has no ambition.

OFFICER	A big boy, yes I am big, I'm bigger than the others. I'm grown up, I've finished school. I've got a knighthood. So why am I sitting here? Haven't I just been given a knighthood?
TEACHER	Yes but you have to sit here until you get a sense of responsibility.
OFFICER	Yes, you have to be responsible. Twice two . . . equals two and I can prove that by analogy. One times one is one. So two times two is two.
TEACHER	Logical but wrong.
OFFICER	Logic can't be wrong. Let's try again. One goes into one once. So two goes into two twice.
TEACHER	Then what's one times three?
OFFICER	Three.
TEACHER	And it follows logically that two times three is also three.
OFFICER	No, that can't be right . . . it can't be . . . or perhaps . . . No, I haven't got a sense of responsibility.
TEACHER	You certainly haven't.
OFFICER	So how long do I have to go on sitting here?
TEACHER	How long? Do you believe time and space exist? If time exists, you should be able to say what it is. What's time?
OFFICER	Time? I can't exactly say but I know what it is. So I can know what twice two is and not be able to say it. Can you tell me what time is?

TEACHER	Of course.
BOYS	Then say it.
TEACHER	Time flies while we speak. So time is something that flies while I'm speaking.
BOY	You're speaking now and I'm going to fly, so I'm time.

BOY *flies*.

TEACHER	That's certainly logical.
OFFICER	But it must be wrong because he can't be time.
TEACHER	That's logical.
OFFICER	So logically, logic must be wrong.
TEACHER	But if logic's wrong, everything's crazy and how can I teach it?
OFFICER	You can't, you're an old idiot.
TEACHER	Don't be impertinent.
OFFICER	I'm an officer, I'm an officer, and I don't see why I'm sitting here with schoolboys getting told off.
TEACHER	Where's your sense of responsibility?

QUARANTINE MASTER *enters*.

Q MASTER	The quarantine's beginning.
OFFICER	He's making me learn my tables and I've got a knighthood.
Q MASTER	So why don't you leave?
OFFICER	I can't.
TEACHER	I thought not. Try.

OFFICER	Save me. Save me from his eyes.
Q MASTER	Come on then. Come and help us dance. We must have a dance before the plague breaks out.
OFFICER	And after that the warship's going to sail?
Q MASTER	It's going to sail first. There'll be tears.
OFFICER	There's always tears. When it goes and when it comes back. Let's go.

They leave TEACHER *teaching.*

MAIDS *and* EDITH *go sadly to the jetty.*

AGNES, OFFICER, QUARANTINE MASTER.

AGNES	This is paradise. But isn't anyone happy here?
OFFICER	Yes, listen. They've just got married.

Enter NEWLYWEDS.

HUSBAND	I'm so happy I could die.
WIFE	Die? why?
HUSBAND	Because bliss burns out. And that means I can't bear it.
WIFE	Let's die together. Now.
HUSBAND	Die? Yes. Because I'm frightened of happiness.

They go.

AGNES	People are so fucked up.
OFFICER	Tell me about it.
	Now here's somebody everyone wants to be.

Enter BLIND MAN.

He owns a hundred villas, he owns the whole coast. All the beaches, forests, all the fish in the sea, birds in the air, animals in the woods. Thousands of people pay him rent and the sun rises over his waves and sets over his hills.

AGNES   And I suppose he thinks he's got something to complain about?

OFFICER   He does because he can't see.

Q MASTER   He's blind.

AGNES   The one they want to be.

OFFICER   He's come to wave goodbye to the warship, his son's on it.

BLIND MAN   I can't see but I can hear. I can hear the anchor tearing the seabed like when you tear a fishhook out of a fish and the heart comes out of its throat. My son's being sent overseas. I can't go with him except in my thoughts. The chains are squeaking . . . and something's fluttering . . . wet handkerchiefs . . . and there's sobbing and sniffing, but it could be the small waves against the nets . . . but it could be the girls on the beach, the girls they've left behind them. I once asked a child whose father was at sea why the sea was salt, and he said because sailors cry. Why do they cry? Because they're so far away. And they put their handkerchiefs on the masts to dry. So then I asked him why do people cry when they're sad? And he said because they have to wash their eyes so they can see better.

Ship sails. GIRLS *waving sadly.*

Signal flag with red raised on the ship. ALICE
waves happily.

AGNES   What does the flag mean?

OFFICER   It means yes. It's the lieutenant's yes in red,
               like blood on the sky's blue uniform.

AGNES   What's no?

OFFICER   Blue like the sick blood in his veins. See
               how happy Alice is.

AGNES   And how Edith's crying.

BLIND MAN   I met his mother and she left me. I still had
               my son and now he's gone too.

AGNES   But I'm sure he'll come back.

BLIND MAN   Who's that? I've heard that voice in my
               dreams. I used to hear it on the first day of
               the summer holidays. I heard it the first
               time I made love to my wife. I heard it the
               night my son was born. It's like a south
               wind. It's like angels.

               SOLICITOR *enters and whispers to* BLIND
               MAN.

               I see.

SOLICITOR   Yes, that's the sort of person she is.

               Right, Agnes, you've seen a lot but you
               haven't tried the worst yet.

AGNES   What's that?

SOLICITOR   Repetition. Going back. Doing it all over
               again. Come on.

AGNES   Where?

SOLICITOR   To your duties.

AGNES	What duties?
SOLICITOR	Everything you always hated.
AGNES	The lentils and dirty clothes?
SOLICITOR	Yes, it's washday and we're washing the handkerchiefs.
AGNES	Do I have to do it all over again?
SOLICITOR	Life's all repetition. Look at the teacher. Right, let's go home.
AGNES	I'd rather be dead.
SOLICITOR	Yes but you're not allowed to kill yourself. It's against the law and you don't get a proper funeral and then you're damned.
AGNES	I'm finding it really hard being a person.
ALL	See.
AGNES	I'm not coming. I want to stay here. Compared to life with you, this is paradise.
	Two BUILDING WORKERS.
BW1	This is hell.
BW2	Forty degrees in the shade.
BW1	Shall we go for a swim?
BW2	We'll be arrested. We can't swim here.
BW1	We could pick some fruit.
BW2	No, we'll be arrested.
BW1	I'm not working in this heat. I'm off.
BW2	You'll be arrested. And anyway you'll starve.
BW1	(*To* AGNES.) So, what do you think? What's your answer?

AGNES	I'm not sure yet. Is it true they're not allowed to swim here?
SOLICITOR	They can try to drown themselves. But then they get beaten up at the police station.
AGNES	Can't they go further down the coast and swim in the countryside?
SOLICITOR	It's all fenced off.
AGNES	No, I mean where it doesn't belong to anyone.
SOLICITOR	It all belongs to someone.
AGNES	But not the sea?
SOLICITOR	Everything. You can't moor a boat without being charged for it. Good, isn't it?
AGNES	Why don't people do something about it?
SOLICITOR	Some of them do but they end up in prison or a psychiatric ward.
AGNES	Who puts them in prison?
SOLICITOR	The great and the good, the law-abiding citizens and the hard-working families.
AGNES	Who puts them in the psychiatric ward?
SOLICITOR	Their own despair.
AGNES	Maybe it has to be like this.
SOLICITOR	That's exactly what some people think.

GENTLEMAN *and* LADY *cross.*

LADY	Are you coming to play cards?
GENT	No, I need some exercise so I can eat dinner.

SOLICITOR   Please don't think I'm a socialist but does
              there have to be such a big difference?

AGNES   It isn't paradise.

SOLICITOR   So come back with me.

AGNES   No, I'm not going back to dirt and lentils
              and arguments. I want to go back where I
              came from. But first we've got to get the
              door open. I want them to open the door.

SOLICITOR   Then you have to go back the way you
              came and go through everything again.

AGNES   All right, if I have to. But first I'm going
              somewhere quiet where there's no people
              because I'm confused. I will see you later.
              (*To* WRITER.) Come with me.

9. Cave

AGNES, WRITER.

WRITER   Where have you brought me?

AGNES   Away from all that. To the edge of the
              world. To a cave where the gods listen to
              people's complaints.

WRITER   How? Here?

AGNES   Look, the cave's shaped like a shell. And an
              ear is shaped like a shell. You know how
              you can listen to a shell and hear the sound
              of your own blood and the thoughts in
              your brain? So if you can hear that in a
              small shell, imagine what you can hear in
              this big one.

WRITER   I can only hear the wind.

AGNES   I'll tell you what it's saying.
             Over the cities
             with their foul smoke and
             over the sea to
             wash our dusty feet
             and shake out our wings.
             People aren't evil
             and people aren't good.
             They live how they can
             one day at a time.
             They come out of dust
             they go back to dust,
             dusty feet, no wings,
             and whose fault is that?

WRITER   I've heard this before.

AGNES   Sh. The winds are still singing.
             Hear us in autumn
             crying down chimneys
             or moaning through the
             cracks of windows, when
             the rain's beating down.
             Hear us in winter
             in forests in the
             snow, at sea hear us
             in the ship's rigging.
             We learnt to howl from
             people, we heard them
             in bed sick, on the
             ground in a battle,
             we heard their pain and
             that's why we're wailing.

WRITER   I thought I . . .

AGNES   Sh. Now the waves are singing.
             We rock the winds to
             sleep, like wet flames we
             burn quench make destroy,
             rocking them to sleep.

Look what's been washed up from wrecked ships. Rowlocks. Bailers. A lifejacket. And part of a guided-missile launcher.

WRITER   Here's a nameboard. Enduring Freedom. That's from the ship we saw sail with the blind man's son. And the lieutenant Alice and Edith loved.

AGNES   Didn't I dream all that? There was a blind man and Alice and Edith. And the quarantine and the sulphur and the honours and the solicitor and Victoria and the tower and the officer . . . I dreamt that.

WRITER   I wrote it.

AGNES   Then you know what poetry is.

WRITER   I know what a dream is. What's poetry?

AGNES   It's not real but maybe it's more than real. It's dreaming while you're awake.

WRITER   Everyone thinks it's playing and nonsense.

AGNES   That's just as well or everyone would lie about and you'd never even have invented agriculture.

WRITER   It's easy for you to say. You don't belong here, you belong in the sky.

AGNES   Yes, I've been here too long. I can't fly any more. (*Raises her arms.*) I'm sinking. (*To gods.*) Help me. (*Silence.*) I can't hear anything any more. I've lost contact. I'm stuck here.

WRITER   Were you planning to . . . go up soon?

AGNES   I'll have to burn off the dust. It won't wash off in the sea. Why?

WRITER   Because I have a sort of petition.

AGNES	What about?
WRITER	From all us people to god, the gods, whatever.
AGNES	And you want me to . . . ?
WRITER	Take it with you.
AGNES	Will you say it?
WRITER	Yes, all right.
AGNES	Say it then.
WRITER	I'd rather hear you say it.
AGNES	How can I read it?
WRITER	Read my mind.
AGNES	Yes, I'll say it.

Why does it hurt to
give birth? why do babies
cry? why are we just
animals and not gods?

Sh. No one understands what life is.

We race over stones
and thistles, if we pick
flowers they're someone
else's, if we're happy
it makes someone sad,
if we're sad it doesn't
make them happier.
And then we just die.
This isn't a good tone to take with
gods.

WRITER   How can I find words
to tell them what it's like?
Put it your own way.

AGNES   Yes, I'll try.

WRITER   What's floating over there? Is it a buoy to
             warn the ships?

AGNES   Yes, it sings when there's danger.

WRITER   I think the sea's rising now. I can hear
             the waves thundering. And what's that?
             A ship . . . on the rocks. Shouldn't the
             buoy be making some sort of noise? Look,
             the sea's rising. We're going to be trapped
             in the cave. That's the ship's siren. It's
             going to be wrecked. The buoy –

             Buoy sound.

             The crew's waving to us. But we're going to
             die too.

AGNES   Don't you want to be released from this
             terrible life?

WRITER   Yes of course but not now. Not in the
             water.

             CREW *on ship singing.*

CREW   Christ our Lord.

WRITER   No one can hear them.

AGNES   Who's that out there?

WRITER   Walking on the water? There's only one
             person who's ever done that.

CREW   Christ our Lord?

AGNES   Is that him?

WRITER   It is, it is, it's the one who was crucified.

AGNES   Why was he crucified?

WRITER   Because he wanted to set people free, I think.

AGNES   Who wanted to crucify him?

WRITER   The great and the good, the law-abiding
             citizens and the hard-working families.

AGNES   This world is so odd.

WRITER   The sea's rising. It's dark. The storm's
             getting up.

             CREW *scream.*

             And the crew are screaming with terror.
             They've seen him walking on the water to
             save them and they're so terrified they're
             jumping overboard. Now they're screaming
             because they're going to die.

             Waves threaten to drown AGNES *and*
             WRITER *in the cave.*

AGNES   If I could be sure it was a ship . . .

WRITER   You know . . . I don't think it is a ship. It's
             a house with trees outside . . . and a
             telephone tower . . . a tower that goes right
             up into the sky. A tower with wires to take
             messages to the gods.

AGNES   They don't need wires.

WRITER   No, it's not a house, not a telephone tower,
             can you see it?

AGNES   What do you see?

WRITER   It's a plain covered with snow. It's the
             army's training ground. The sun's shining
             behind a church and the spire's shadow's
             on the snow. Here come the soldiers.
             They're marching on the church, marching
             up the spire, I think the one who steps on
             the weathercock's going to die. They're
             getting nearer. The corporal's leading them.

Haha. Here comes the shadow of a cloud
rushing across, blots it all out, the steeple's
shadow's gone.

10. Outside the Stage Door

AGNES, OFFICER, STAGE DOOR KEEPER.

AGNES   Have the great and the good arrived yet?

SD KEEPER   Not yet.

AGNES   Then call them at once because we've got
                  to open the door. Everyone thinks the
                  meaning of life is in there.

                  STAGE DOOR KEEPER *blows whistle.*

                  And don't forget the glazier with his
                  diamond.

                  THEATRE PEOPLE *enter.*

                  OFFICER *enters with roses, as at the beginning.*

OFFICER   Victoria!

SD KEEPER   She'll be right down.

OFFICER   That's good. The taxi's waiting, I've booked
                  a table, the champagne's on ice. I have to
                  give you a hug. (*He hugs* STAGE DOOR
                  KEEPER.) Victoria!

VICTORIA   (*Off.*) Coming.

OFFICER   Good. I'll wait.

WRITER   You know that feeling that something's
                  happened before.

AGNES   Yes, me too.

WRITER	Maybe I dreamt it.
AGNES	Or wrote it?
WRITER	Or wrote it.
AGNES	Then you know what poetry is.
WRITER	I know what a dream is.
AGNES	I think we've said this before too.
WRITER	You'll soon be able to work out what reality is.
AGNES	Or dreaming.
WRITER	Or poetry.

Enter CHAIRMAN OF INQUIRY, BISHOP, PSYCHOANALYST, SCIENTIST *and* BARRISTER.

CHAIR	I am here to chair an inquiry into the opening of the door. What do you think, bishop?
BISHOP	I don't think, I believe, and I believe the door should not be opened because it conceals a dangerous truth.
PSYCH	The patient fears the truth. And the analyst helps him live with it. In an ordinary unhappy way.
SCIENTIST	What is 'the truth'? Forty-six chromosomes. Thirty thousand genes.
BARRISTER	It's what I can prove beyond a reasonable doubt.
PSYCH	Truth is what you discover about yourself after years of lying on the couch.
SCIENTIST	That's not scientific truth. It's talk.

BISHOP *cheers.*

PSYCH
What are you cheering for? you hate science. You think the world was made in six days ten thousand years ago.

SCIENTIST *cheers.*

BISHOP
What are you cheering for? You only know what's under your microscope. Our truth is always true and yours constantly changes.

SCIENTIST
Idiot.

Fight.

CHAIR
The truth is outside the terms of reference of this inquiry. Perhaps we should move to the opening of the door.

BISHOP
I am the way, the truth and the light.

PSYCH
The Oedipus complex.

SCIENTIST
The prefrontal cortex.

BARRISTER
Prove it, prove it, prove it.

ALL
(*Cheer.*) The door's open.

CHAIR
What's behind the door?

GLAZIER
I can't see anything.

CHAIR
No, he might not perhaps be capable. Bishop, what's behind the door?

BISHOP
Nothing. That's the answer. God created everything out of nothing.

PSYCH
The feeling of nothingness can be a symptom of −

SCIENTIST
There's simply nothing there.

OFFICER
Nothing there?

BARRISTER	I doubt that. This is a case of conspiracy to deceive. I appeal to the great and the good, the law-abiding citizens and the hard-working families.
ALL	We've been deceived.
CHAIR	Who has deceived you?
ALL	She has.
CHAIR	What did you mean by opening the door?
AGNES	If I told you, you wouldn't believe me.
SCIENTIST	The simple fact is there's nothing there.
AGNES	Nothing at all. But you don't understand it.
SCIENTIST	What is there to understand? It's a load of bollocks.
ALL	Bollocks. Get her.
BARRISTER	I grant you a conditional discharge provided you leave the country. You can go back where you came from. With what you got out of it.
AGNES	(*To* WRITER.) I'm sorry for them.
WRITER	Are you serious?
AGNES	Always serious.
WRITER	Sorry for the hard-working families, the law-abiding citizens and the great and the good?
AGNES	Them most of all. But what did he mean, what I got out of it?
WRITER	Don't worry about it. He was just talking.
AGNES	What I got out of coming to earth? I'm hurt by that.
WRITER	That's why he said it.

AGNES	Yes but –
ALL	She refuses to answer.
CHAIR	Get her.
AGNES	I've already answered.
ALL	She thinks she knows the answer, get her.
AGNES	Come on and I'll – a long way away – I'll tell you the secret where no one can see us or hear us. Because –

SOLICITOR *enters.*

SOLICITOR	Have you forgotten your duties?
AGNES	No. But I have higher duties.
SOLICITOR	And your daughter?
AGNES	My daughter. Anything else?
SOLICITOR	She's crying for you.
AGNES	This pain, what is it?
SOLICITOR	Don't you know?
AGNES	No.
SOLICITOR	Conscience.
AGNES	Conscience?
SOLICITOR	Yes and you'll get it every time you hurt someone else.
AGNES	Isn't there a cure?
SOLICITOR	Do your duty.
AGNES	What if I've got two duties?
SOLICITOR	Do one first, then the other.
AGNES	The highest first. So you look after our daughter, and I'll do my duty.

SOLICITOR   She misses you. Don't you understand?
             someone is suffering because of you.

AGNES   Now I'm torn in two.

SOLICITOR   This is one of life's little troubles, you see?

AGNES   It hurts.

WRITER   If you knew what grief I'd caused, you
             wouldn't want to hold my hand.

AGNES   Why? what?

WRITER   I did what I felt was my duty to my
             vocation and completely fucked up
             everyone who loved me. I gave my father a
             heart attack, my mother a nervous
             breakdown and stopped seeing my best
             friend because he was exploiting the people
             I was writing for. And it's no help thinking
             you did the right thing because next minute
             you think you were wrong. That's what
             life's like.

AGNES   Come with me.

SOLICITOR   You have a child.

AGNES   Goodbye.

11. Outside the Tower

*Like the first scene, except the flowers are now bluebells. A
chrysanthemum bud on top of the tower is about to open.*

AGNES *and* WRITER.

AGNES   Soon I'm going up out of this world. I'll
             use fire. It's what you call dying and you're
             frightened of it.

WRITER	It's fear of the unknown.
AGNES	But you do know. Have you always doubted everything?
WRITER	No, sometimes I'm certain of something. Then it goes again. Like a dream when you wake up.
AGNES	It's not easy being alive.
WRITER	You know that now?
AGNES	Yes, I do now.
WRITER	But weren't you going to tell me the answer to whatever the question is.
AGNES	What's the point? You don't believe what you're told.
WRITER	I will believe you because I know who you are.
AGNES	All right, listen. (*Whispers.*)
WRITER	My dream.
	AGNES *whispers.*
	And then ?
	AGNES *whispers.*
	What about peace? and rest?
AGNES	Don't ask any more. I can't say any more. Because everything's ready for my death. Flowers. Candles. White sheets over the windows. And the fire.
WRITER	Why are you so calm? Are you someone who can't feel pain?
AGNES	I've felt yours. I've felt everyone's.

WRITER	Tell me what you've felt.
AGNES	Could you tell me? Could words ever do it?
WRITER	No, words are useless. I've always known what I write doesn't say what I mean so when I get praised I feel ashamed.
AGNES	Look into my eyes.
WRITER	I can't bear it.
AGNES	Then how would you bear my words if I spoke my own language?
WRITER	But tell me before you go. What was the worst thing about being down here?
AGNES	Just existing. Knowing my sight was blurred by my eyes, my hearing dulled by my ears, and my bright thought trapped in the grey maze of a brain. Have you seen a brain?
WRITER	And you're telling me that's what's wrong with us? How else can we be?
AGNES	First I'll get rid of the dust on my feet.

Puts shoes on fire.

Others enter, put things on fire, go.

SD KEEPER	Do you mind if I burn my coat?
OFFICER	My roses. Well, thorns, really.
BILLSTICK	The posters can go but not my net.
GLAZIER	The diamond which opened the door. Goodbye.
SOLICITOR	My great lawsuit about asbestos poisoning.
Q MASTER	A small contribution, my monster mask.
VICTORIA	My beauty, my sadness.
EDITH	My ugliness, my sadness.

BLIND MAN	My hands were my eyes.
WRITER	Sometimes when you're about to die, isn't your whole life meant to go past you in a flash? Is this it?
AGNES	It is for me. Goodbye.
WRITER	What about last words?
AGNES	I can't. Emotions don't fit into words.

KRISTIN *enters*.

KRISTIN	Pasting, pasting, till there's nothing left to paste.
WRITER	And if heaven cracked open you'd paste it shut. Go away.
KRISTIN	Aren't there some windows for me in the tower?
WRITER	No, Kristin.
KRISTIN	Then I'll go.

KRISTIN *goes*.

AGNES   Goodbye, this is the
end, goodbye writer,
you live well floating
in the air, plunging
into the mud but
not getting stuck there.

When you're leaving you
love what you've lost and
you're sorry for what
you've done and far more
what you didn't do.
I know what it's like.
You want to stay and
you want to go and

Goodbye. Tell people
I won't forget them.
I'll tell the gods
what being alive is.
Because I'm sorry.
Goodbye.

She goes into the tower.

The tower burns.

The bud bursts into a giant chrysanthemum.

End.